CUT
THE
CRAP!

A YORKSHIRE MAN'S A-TO-Z GUIDE
TO MINDFULNESS

Rick Parcell

9009816346

Please return/renew this item by the last date shown.
Items may also be renewed by the internet*

https://library.eastriding.gov.uk

* Please note a PIN will be required to access this service
- this can be obtained from your library

CUT
THE
CRAP!

A YORKSHIRE MAN'S A-TO-Z GUIDE
TO MINDFULNESS

Rick Parcell

A – AWARENESS

What is awareness?

Awareness is simply mindfulness. It's a state of being in which a person can see everything that goes on around them more clearly. They relax into the present moment and focus more fully on the people around them and the environment they are in. Awareness is the key to change, and the only way to change something is to become aware of it. After all, if you are not conscious of a habit, then how can you change it?

Have you ever noticed how the brain filters information? It does this in a certain way. If someone said to you, "Look for all the blue things around you", you would focus on blue. There could be green fields around you but they would fade into the background. By becoming aware of what we focus on, we begin to realise we can change the way we look at things and thus have more control over our own reactions and decisions.

Where does awareness come from?

Awareness can be found any time you stop and recognise your own thought processes. It's pure consciousness. Meditation is one good way to become aware of your thoughts.

Another way to develop awareness is by choosing to be aware of the food you are chewing, instead, for example, of eating mindlessly whilst watching television.

Why does it help to gain awareness?

Awareness can lead to minor changes in life, which cumulatively make a big difference over time. An example would be becoming aware of how you can affect people with your language every day and how much positivity you bring to other people's lives – or indeed negativity!

Awareness also puts us more in control of our emotions and behaviour – two key aspects of our being that shape the course of our lives.

How can you use awareness?

You can become aware of the following things:
How you use food – is it for emotional reasons or as good fuel for the mind and body?
How much water you drink and whether you drink sugary drinks and/or alcohol too often;
How you talk to yourself (your self-talk) and

others; which of your daily habits serve you and which aspects of your behaviour do not.

FUNWORK

List three areas of thought that are not serving you and that you would like to change. For example: I feel lonely and empty inside – I eat chocolate. I need confidence – I drink alcohol.

1. _____

2. _____

3. _____

How could changing these affect your life right now and what positive consequences would there be? Write this down for each one.

1. _____

_____

2. _____

_____

3. _____

_____

B – BELIEFS

What are beliefs?

Beliefs can influence our daily decisions as they are things that we consider to be true without giving a second thought to. They can be as simple as "I am unhealthy" or "I am fat" or as far-reaching as "I believe in God". They can change the course of our lives and actions in so many different ways.

Where do beliefs come from?

They come from external sources, such as religious groups, education, family, friends and culture, or from internal sources, such as the unconscious mind. If we are unaware of these beliefs, we simply can't change them.

Why do beliefs have power over us?

They have power over us because they can determine the direction of our life, our daily decisions and our interactions with people. Beliefs that have been passed on through previous generations or via our family can create traditions that have to be followed. For example, "I believe that no one in my family is any good at sport." People who believe this will often be unfit because they don't feel motivated to take exercise.

How can you use beliefs?

We can use healthy beliefs to enable our unconscious mind to support our decisions. For example, if a person thinks that they can't lose weight, they will be less likely to make the effort to eat healthy food. Another person could choose to believe that they can be fit and healthy and thus begin to eat in a healthy way and make better decisions around food.

FUNWORK

List three beliefs that are not serving you and which you want to become more aware of in your day-to-day life.

1. _____
2. _____
3. _____

How are these beliefs affecting your life? Write down how each one affects your life right now and what the consequences of this are.

1. _____

_____

2. _____

_____

3. _____

_____

C – CAUSE AND EFFECT

What are cause and effect?
Cause and effect are relevant to everyone we know, everything we do and everywhere we go. "Cause and effect" is a universal rule and applies to everything we come into contact with in life. Think of throwing a stone into a pond: as the stone hits the water, it makes a splash and causes ripples that continue for several moments, moving outwards and becoming larger, way across the pond. In the same way, everything we do has consequences.

Where do cause and effect influence us?
Cause and effect have a huge influence on our lives. Every time we eat, we are at cause. Every time we open our mouths and say something, we are at cause. When we choose to drink something we are at cause. Every time we think, we are at cause at that very moment.

Why do cause and effect matter?
Basically we all need to continue to remember that we are never a victim – only the victim of our own thought processes. We are always at cause in our world in one way or another and

are responsible for 90 per cent of the outcomes of our lives. Just 10 per cent is out of our control – such as other people's words or actions, or the actions of the government. However, how we respond to other people's actions or behaviour, or to external circumstances, is within our control. Therefore we really have 95 per cent of control of our world.

Note: "Response – ability" is what responsibility really means. The ability to respond in the best way possible, given the circumstances.

How can you use cause and effect in daily life?
We can use cause and effect in our daily lives by being aware of the fact that every choice we make in life helps determine our future and by knowing that we must take full responsibility for our decisions. Food does not make you overweight – we are all at cause when we are at the dinner table or the buffet! No one is forcing food down our throats. The same goes for alcohol. Just because we are in a bar, it does not mean that we have to drink alcohol. There are many non-alcoholic choices and virgin cocktails nowadays and friends do not usually force us physically to drink...we have a choice – we are at cause!

When can you use cause and effect?

We can use cause and effect when we are making choices which involve food or alcohol, or as we respond to different situations we find ourselves in, or when people say things that affect us. By becoming mindful of the power of cause, we begin to understand the long-term consequences of our actions.

FUNWORK

Think of three areas of your life in which your attitudes and actions generally have negative consequences. Write them down.

1. _____

_____

2. _____

_____

3. _____

_____

Why are you currently making these three choices and how do you need to change them?

1. _____
   _____
   _____

2. _____
   _____
   _____

3. _____
   _____
   _____

D - DAILY HABITS

What are daily habits?
Daily habits are used every day in life. A classic example is brushing your teeth. Most of us do this without thinking.

Where do your daily habits come from?
We learn many of our habits from our parents and teachers during childhood. Others may be picked up from our friends and our society. Eventually, they become ingrained within us and we become unconscious of them – unless we think about them and become aware of them.

After many years, habits can become "second nature". Therefore it's important for all habits to be chosen wisely and consciously, ensuring they are always geared towards positive outcomes for our health and other aspects of our lives.

Why do daily habits have power over us?
They have power over us because they create a "compound effect". Over a period of time they have a huge impact on our lives, and if negative habits (such as smoking, eating too much chocolate, drinking too much alcohol, etc.) are

allowed to build up, they can become highly addictive "go-to methods" in times of stress.

How can you use these habits?

We can use daily habits to help us lead a healthier and happier life, by consciously cultivating good ones and building them into our daily life where possible. Just eating one salad a day for the rest of your life would have massive consequences for your well-being. If you then added in drinking a large bottle of water a day, you would have integrated two positive daily habits into your routine easily.

FUNWORK

List three positive daily habits you could adopt now and commit yourself to for the rest of your life.

1. _____

_____

2. _____

_____

3. _____

_____

E – EMOTIONS

What are emotions?

Emotions are feelings. They have the power to affect our attitudes to food, alcohol, relationships (with others and ourselves) and other aspects of our lives. They can also have an impact on our thoughts, desires and impulses.

Where do your emotions come from?

Emotions come from the heart, though they are influenced by our mind, and they have a lot of power over us. They are a very human part of us and it's important to recognise them as much as possible.

Why do emotions affect us?

They affect us because we are human. Most people believe they have no power to help themselves feel better, and in some cases this can have negative consequences. However, we can change the way we feel. Why do people go to the cinema? To feel an emotion. Films can elicit sadness or laughter from us and make us cry. Some people even like the feeling of being frightened or horrified, as it may help them get in touch with their emotions. Drinking alcohol is another way of establishing a kind of contact with our emotions, though it can also be used to escape from difficult feelings. Some people bury emotions with food or eat to feel full if they feel numb emotionally.

How can you use your emotions in your daily life?

Emotions can be used to your advantage – when we feel the urge to eat, we can choose consciously to eat something natural or healthy. We can learn to use our emotions in the right way. For example, fear can be turned into adrenaline in a situation where someone needs to overcome their stage-fright or speak in front of a group. When we feel sad, we could begin the habit of mindfully drinking water, instead of reaching for a glass of wine to suppress what we are feeling. Similarly, going for a long walk after a frustrating argument with a loved one is a positive way to manage negative feelings.

FUNWORK

Write down the emotion that you feel the most in your daily life. Is it love, gratitude, hate, anxiety, or something else?

1. _____

Answer on two lines how two emotions you feel on a regular basis influence your attitudes to food and alcohol?

1. _____

   _____

2. _____

   _____

Draw the emotion you feel right now:

F – FOCUS

What is focus?

Although about seventy thousand thoughts go through our mind each day, current theories suggest that our conscious mind can only focus on three to seven things at any one time. Focus is the ability to choose one thing at a time from the conscious mind, then think and act on only that in the moment we are in. **Remember – where focus goes, energy flows!**

Where does focus come from?

Focus comes from the conscious mind – the part of the mind we use to concentrate on something or someone in the present moment. An example would be that right now you are using your conscious mind to read and focus on these words, while your unconscious mind is working on your breathing and holding all your memories for you to access whenever you need them.

Why does focus affect you?

Focus affects us in many ways. We now live in the information age, and with so much stimulus affecting our brains in the twenty-first century, focus is becoming increasingly important because there are so many distractions.

What we focus on affects what we feel in each moment. Therefore, if we focus on things that will make us happy in the long term, we will experience more positive emotions. If we focus on our problems, we will experience more negative emotions

How can you use focus daily?

Focus can be very useful for goal-setting. If we narrow down what's really important to us and identify our most important goal, we will achieve it more quickly and more easily.

Here's an example. "I want to lose weight". A much more focused goal would be "I am going to have only 10 per cent body fat by 1st June 2018 because I want to feel more confident and not worry about my weight. I understand it's more important to have muscle than to be light, because muscle is denser than fat. I hope that this positive mindset and improved physique will help me to meet my future wife/husband!"

FUNWORK

Name three things that your focus must be on for you to be happy within yourself on a daily basis.

1. _____

2. _____

3. _____

G – GOAL-SETTING

What is goal-setting?
Goal-setting is a process for achieving any dream you can think of in your life. It's critical in life to feel a sense of purpose every day, and to have things to strive for and destinations to reach.

Where does goal-setting come from?
Goal-setting has been used for many years and has been a major tool for many successful people. It comes from the conscious mind and it's a choice. The trick is to help the unconscious mind believe it can achieve the goals. The unconscious mind has developed over two million years to protect you and help you survive. To do this, it sometimes resists the conscious mind by putting up various walls and barriers. When it starts to believe that it will benefit from a chosen goal, it will drop its barriers and walls to make the dream come true. An example would be overcoming a fear of heights. The unconscious mind may have programmed you to be afraid of leaving your job, even if you hate it and find it very stressful. Once the unconscious mind is convinced you will survive even if you

take this risk, it will let the conscious mind choose to apply for new jobs and allow you to shine in interviews.

Why does goal-setting work?

It works because the conscious mind can visualise whatever or wherever you wish to get to in life. By using the conscious mind to create these visions, you can help make the unconscious mind believe it's possible.

How can you use goal-setting?

Goal-setting can be used in all areas of your life – and specificity is critical. Here is a question for you: Have you ever said to a taxi driver "Take me anywhere". Or would you normally say something like "Take me to 123 Cool Street in Covent Garden". The unconscious mind will follow any order received from the conscious mind, as long as there is good communication between the two, the unconscious understands it's safe to do so and there is a big enough "why" or purpose.

FUNWORK

Set goals in the following three areas and be as specific as possible. (For example: I will have only 10 per cent body fat and be dress size 14 by 1st Feb 2018 because I will look and feel better in my new bikini.)

Health

_____

_____

_____

_____

Career

_____

_____

_____

_____

Relationships

_____

_____

_____

_____

H – HOME STATE

What is your home state?
Your home state is the emotional place in which you spend 80 per cent of your time in your mind. Are you in a grateful state of mind, in which you have a sense of the world's abundance moment to moment, or a scarcity-based state of mind, in which you feel that there is not enough (love, money, etc.) to go around?

Where do home states come from?
Home states come from the unconscious mind – it has a "go-to" setting which has been developed from years of experience. This state is often not thought about unless we become aware of it. Some people come from a place of calm, frustration and anger or chronic suffering.

Why is a home state important?
This home state is important because it will affect how we feel, think and act most of the time.

How can you use your home state and make it a good one?

We can take control of our lives and have full power over our decisions more often if we become aware of our home state and how long we spend in it. There are many ways to get into a helpful, positive home state. Here are a few:

Listening to music
Dancing with friends
Workouts
Meditation
Yoga
Breath and gratitude work

FUNWORK

Identify your home state. What do you think it is and how much time do you spend there?

_____

_____

_____

_____

_____

_____

What bad decisions have you made from this state of mind in the past?

_____

_____

_____

_____

_____

What new home state are you choosing to be in and how will you gain access to it whenever you want to?

_____

_____

_____

_____

_____

I – IDENTITY

What is an identity?

Our sense of identity is critical to who we are. It defines us. The words we use and the way we look are a direct result of how we see ourselves –our identity. However, because we perform different roles in life, we are constantly switching identity and these identities all hold different powers for us to use (parent / educator / listener / sportsperson / lover / good friend, etc.). For example, when we act as a parent, we act as a good role model to children. If we are playing tennis, we imagine ourselves as a great tennis player. If we see our identity as being someone who cares about ourselves and others, we will act accordingly and stay healthy.

Where does identity come from?

Identity comes from our beliefs, our character, the lessons we've learnt in life, our culture and our parents. We put all these experiences and this learning together and they form our identity. We communicate it to the world through our words and actions.

Why does identity matter?

It matters because all our actions and decisions in our life are being led by how we see ourselves – our identity. For example, if you see yourself as an environmentalist, you may dress that way, eat that way and behave that way – embracing nature.

How can you use identity?

Identity can be used in daily life to great effect. For example, if you see yourself as a teacher, you can choose to be a role model and dress accordingly. Your body language will be strong and purposeful and you will find ways of helping people learn.

FUNWORK

Choose your identity now. Be as detailed as possible. What do you see, hear and feel? (For example, I am a healthy person, who listens to everyone, is kind and always does their best.)

What is your ideal self?

_____

_____

_____

Name a strong point in your identity. Why do you see this as a strength?

_____

_____

_____

Name a weakness in your identity that you would like to change for the better?

_____

_____

_____

Draw your ideal self:

J – JUST WORDS

What are words?
Your words create your life – it's that simple. If a person does not know many words, this can limit them. The words we use every day have a direct effect on the meaning our experiences have for us, the memories we generate, our interactions with people and most importantly, our dealings with ourselves. By becoming mindful of the words that we use, we can make much better choices and change the outcomes in our life. Words are very empowering.

Where do words come from?
Words come from our education, our experiences, our environment, our culture and our parents. They are absorbed and then used in daily life in all our thinking and the situations we find ourselves in. The fewer words we have stored in the unconscious mind, the less chance we have of empowering ourselves each day because we limit our experience with a narrow range of personal language.

Why do words matter?

Words matter because they affect our thoughts and feelings every single day. Having a richer vocabulary helps us to enjoy life more. Of course, we have to use words thoughtfully. Sometimes we don't pause and take the time to think. We must learn to engage the conscious mind and choose our words more carefully.

How can you use words in a better way?

Every word can be expressed in a positive manner.

Here are some examples:

Sore – My body feels sexier today and is changing shape.

Failure – This is only feedback, telling me how not to do it this way.

Tired – I must recharge and energise myself now.

Can't – I can do this.

Should – "Must" is far more powerful.

Try – This is a **weasel** or "get out of it" word.

Use "I am" or "I am going to" or "I will".

FUNWORK

Identify three words you use on a regular basis (such as "like", "OK", try", etc.) and change them to a more positive word or expression.

1. _____
2. _____
3. _____

Which three words best describe you right now? List them.

1. _____
2. _____
3. _____

List three words that describe your absolute best self.

1. _____
2. _____
3. _____

K – KEEP GOING (= PERSISTENCE)

What is persistence?
Persistence is the ability to keep going, never giving in and never stopping until you reach your goal or target. It's a major factor in the difference between success and lack of success.

Where does persistence come from?
Persistence comes from the conscious mind and also a person's "why" or reason for doing something. When someone has a why, they find it harder to give up because they have a fire that is burning within them. Without this fire, there is no persistence or reason to carry on. Here's a quick question: What would light your fire in the areas of your life in which you give up easily?

Why does persistence matter?
Persistence matters because certain patterns begin to emerge in people who are successful. They don't give up as they are getting near their goal and they never stop until they reach it – indeed they often go way beyond it. Often the people who give up don't realise how close they are to success when they walk away – maybe just moments away. Persistence takes people over the finish line, every time.

How can you be more persistent?

There are ways to be persistent and they are often linked to questions for the unconscious mind. What would happen if you did give up? What would happen if you didn't give up? What would you miss out on if you gave up? These are three classic questions you can ask yourself in the uncertain times in life when you are thinking about not following through.

Examples of persistence:
Being out jogging and beginning to walk is a sign of persistence because you are not stopping, just walking and beginning to enjoy interval workouts instead!

Not passing a job interview is a good sign of persistence because you attended, learned how not to answer the questions and will soon move on to another job interview and get that job!

Not buying those nice shoes is a sign of persistence if you're putting the money towards something that will help you in the longer term, such as a deposit for a flat.

FUNWORK

Think about where you have given up in the past. Now imagine and write down what would have happened if you had persisted.

List three good examples of times when you have used persistence to achieve success in your life. Name the top emotion or human quality you used to help you persist.

1. _____
   _____

2. _____
   _____

3. _____
   _____

L – LIMITING BELIEFS

What are limiting beliefs?
Limiting beliefs hold us back from achieving all the things we want to do in life. Uncovering them is paramount to discovering what is holding us back and what we need to choose to believe about ourselves in order to reach our true potential. An example of a limiting belief would be "I can never complete a marathon". Ask yourself if this is really true. You could walk it and still achieve this.

Where do these beliefs come from?
They come from our education, family, media, culture, memories and previous experiences. They can grow as we get older and our self-talk reinforces them.

Why do limiting beliefs matter?
Limiting beliefs matter because they affect our actions and the choices we make in life. The things we fear in life usually come from limiting beliefs or the unconscious mind, which is always protecting us from harm and helping us survive. An example might be the belief "I will never be able to swim". This might influence our choice

of holiday destination with a loved one or our family and might affect others who want to enjoy the water and who feel safe in it.

How can you use limiting beliefs?

We can use limiting beliefs by first identifying them, and then working on them to reduce their negative impact. We can recognise the fact that they affect our confidence and our ability to do things and enjoy life. Once we become mindful of this fact, we can break down these mind barriers and achieve whatever we set out to do.

FUNWORK

Name three limiting beliefs you hold about yourself. For example: I will never make lots of money.

1. _____

_____

2. _____

_____

3. _____

_____

Now change each one and write down the changed belief. What positive changes would you see in your life if you did change each of these?

1. _____

   _____

2. _____

   _____

3. _____

   _____

M – MOVEMENT

What is movement?
Movement can take the form of weight training, cardiovascular training, TRX training – anything that gets the body moving and breathing a little faster or more deeply, and challenges it in a positive way by taking it slightly out of its normal, stationary comfort zone. Daily movement is vital for the body and ensures that we are able to enjoy life to the full.

Where does movement come from?
Movement comes from the unconscious mind – remember the mind controls the body. If we have gained willpower from a big enough "why" and have a reason to move, we can ensure that we move each day for the rest of our life.

Why does movement matter?
Like a car that is left in a garage for too long, if the body is not used daily, it won't be at its best and will not start up easily! Moving the body each day is important because when air or blood is not being moved around it, there is a possibility that some areas of it will function less well and may break down prematurely.

How can you use movement?

You can you use movement in the best way by ensuring the body is tested every day. The musculoskeletal system, the cardiovascular system and the respiratory system must be used and tested daily – they improve and become more efficient if demands are made of them. Just like a car, we need proper maintenance, regular checks and the appropriate fuel if we are to perform at our best.

FUNWORK

Name one type of movement you can do daily and say at what time of day you can commit to it.

_____

_____

Write down exactly why you would benefit from it.

_____

_____

_____

_____

What are the long-term consequences of your actions?

_____

_____

_____

_____

N – NATURAL FOODS

What are natural foods?
Natural foods are live foods from nature. By live foods, we mean foods that are fresh and don't contain preservatives. Classic examples are fresh fruit and vegetables. **Remember - food is medicine.**

Where do natural foods come from?
They come from nature and not a factory. Natural, live foods provide lots of health benefits. They are usually eaten after minimal cooking or preparation and contain much more life force than dead, processed food, though processed food may sometimes taste better because it often contains a lot of salt, sugar and other addictive substances.

Why eat natural foods?
The human body recognises natural food and is only able to fully digest this type of food. It is not designed to eat much processed food. When we eat natural, live foods, we are making a mindful choice to be good to ourselves. By eating unprocessed food, we ensure that we consume life-giving, nutrient-dense food that the body

truly recognises and is nourished by. Nature's garden provides an abundance of vitamins and minerals that are critical for growth and repair.

How can we use natural foods?
We can use it as daily medicine. Recognising that natural/live food is a medicine that helps to reduce the risk of illness and fights disease within the body, is a very important thing to do from an early age. This enables us to form better habits over a period of time and builds a foundation for life-long health.

FUNWORK
Identify how much of your daily nutrition plan is natural foods. Do you need to switch over? If so, why?

_____

_____

_____

_____

_____

Identity five different types of processed food in your diet right now and explain why you eat each one. Is the processed food feeding an emotion?

1. _____
   _____
   _____

2. _____
   _____
   _____

3. _____
   _____
   _____

4. _____
   _____
   _____

5. _____
   _____
   _____

O – OBSTACLES

What are obstacles?
Obstacles are barriers that are placed in our path by the outside world. Two examples are examinations and job interviews.

Where do obstacles come from?
They come in various shapes and sizes. Ironically, they are shaping us for the good and making us into better versions of ourselves. When we first perceive an obstacle, we can either stand passively by and fear it, or prepare, take it in hand and overcome it. Once we understand how to prepare for the obstacle and decide what action to take, we can leap over it and make "the breakthrough".

Why do obstacles affect us?
Obstacles affect us by placing inhibitions and negative thoughts into the mind which were not previously there. We can believe that obstacles are insuperable, with success waiting agonisingly on the other side. If our values and beliefs are not properly aligned, with our conscious and unconscious minds in harmony, there can be damaging consequences. As well

as not feeling good about ourselves, we may not experience one of the biggest joys in life, "the breakthrough" – the moment when an obstacle is overcome.

How can we use obstacles to better ourselves?
The desire to make progress is a basic human emotion, and satisfying it makes us feel better about how we are spending our life. How we view the obstacles that we encounter has a significant effect on our unconscious mind. If we continue to see obstacles as progress points and look at them as a chance to use all the amazing capabilities inherent in all our minds and bodies, we will reach our true potential. When we see obstacles as a chance to progress in life, we can create new beliefs, build more confidence and learn that we have everything within us now to overcome any obstacle that life presents us with.

FUNWORK

Identify the top three obstacles that are preventing you from making progress in your life right now.

1. _____
2. _____
3. _____

How can you overcome these obstacles and make the "breakthrough" you deserve?

1. _____
   _____
   _____

2. _____
   _____
   _____

3. _____
   _____
   _____

P – PERSONAL POWER

What is personal power?
Personal power is the ability to use the resources you have available at any particular time to make great choices. We have a big influence over the direction of our lives and we have more choice each day than we often think. This is personal power.

Where does personal power come from?
Personal power comes from the ability to get our unconscious mind working for us. The more we use our own powers – our ability to think, act and feel in a positive way – the more we can shape our world.

Why does personal power affect us?
By understanding how it can affect us in a negative way, we can use personal power in a positive way. If we believe we have no control over our lives, we are in danger of being at the mercy of our circumstances. However, when we realise that we have unlimited personal power inside us, we can change the direction of our life.

How can we use personal power?

We can use personal power and know that we are always in control of our internal world. How we react to outside circumstances is up to us. What we focus on, we feel. Therefore it's important to decide what to focus on – it has a big influence on how we feel. This can provide massive personal power because if we are living in a good mood or happy state of mind, we will have much more personal power to use in our daily decision-making.

FUNWORK

Name three areas of your life in which you can use more personal power and of which you can take more ownership.

1. _____
   _____

2. _____
   _____

3. _____
   _____

Q – QUIET

What is quiet?
Quiet is the personal doctor that you can call on any time. It's a healing place that the mind can seek out whenever it needs to recharge, unload stress and feel calm. We live in a loud world full of communication and noise. Therefore it's important never to underestimate the power of quiet.

Where does quiet come from?
It comes from a place that is inside you. It's there all the time. The external world can be very noisy. To go inside ourselves to find inner peace, we need to tap into the source. This source is within us all.

How does quiet affect us?
It affects us in a vital way. When we experience internal mind clutter or external noise pollution, it's difficult for the mind to process information. Once the quiet has helped us into a place of tranquility, through methods such as meditation, conscious breathing or yoga, we can become mindful of our wild thought processes and not be controlled by them.

How can we use quiet?

Quiet can be used to reduce stress, relax the mind and help us become more aware of any thoughts and negative self-talk. It can help reduce blood pressure, lower the heart rate and ease tension around the body.

FUNWORK

Identify a time of day when you can have five to ten minutes of quiet time. Write it down here and put it into your schedule.

_____

Write down three positive things you can take from this quiet time and say why this would benefit you.

1. _____

   _____

2. _____

   _____

3. _____

   _____

R – REST

What is rest?
Rest is when we simply do nothing. We come to a halt and sit down or lie down, letting the mind and body relax and slow down completely.

Where does rest come from?
Rest comes from listening to the instinct or message registering in the brain or within the body that tells us that it is time to slow down or stop what we are doing for a while. It's a call from nature but is often not heard – or is frequently ignored.

Why does rest affect us?
Rest affects us by allowing our overloaded minds and bodies to regain their energy. If we don't listen to our inner voice, we add stress to the body and can get fatigued by continuing with what we are doing. We may even overload the mind or body with stress.

How can we use rest?
We can use rest by allowing our heart rate to slow down, learning to control our breathing and understanding that it is perfectly normal in

the busy world we live in to rest. Animals rest when they need to – our needs are no different. Rest comes in a variety of forms, including sleeping, lying down, stretching, meditation, tai chi or yoga.

FUNWORK

Write down how much rest you give yourself every day.

_____

_____

_____

What type or types of rest will you choose to allow yourself to use from now on?

_____

_____

_____

S – SIMPLICITY

What is simplicity?
Simplicity is the ability we all have within us to keep life as uncomplicated as possible, by making the right decisions and choices, and by not holding on to unnecessary things or building up too many distractions.

Where does simplicity come from?
It comes from knowing what you want, knowing yourself and knowing what you simply don't want or need in your life.

Why does simplicity affect us?
In the busy world we live in today, it's important to keep life as simple as possible. This is because if you focus on just a few things rather than a lot, you have fewer distractions, which enables you to focus on what's most important to you.

How can we use simplicity?
We can use simplicity by identifying exactly what we do and don't want in our lives. An example would be sticking to one body part a day when working out – chest, Monday; legs, Tuesday, etc. – and thus not feeling confused about complicated exercise plans.

FUNWORK

Identify ten things you want to reduce in your life or remove or from it.

1. _____
2. _____
3. _____
4. _____
5. _____
6. _____
7. _____
8. _____
9. _____
10. _____

T – TAKE A BREATH

What is taking a breath?

Taking a breath is all about stopping whatever you are doing and just breathing. It means making a conscious effort to do this because most of the time our breathing is controlled by the unconscious mind.

Where does taking a breath come from?

Taking a breath comes from becoming mindful of our thoughts and our bodies, then becoming aware of the action of our lungs. We do this because we understand it's an important way to return to the moment. When we realise we are only in the now – not the past or the future but the present moment – we can discover the moment we are in and enjoy the breath.

Why does taking a breath mean so much to us?

Taking a breath means so much to us simply because without the breath there is no life. In fact four minutes is about the time we can survive without air, without becoming brain damaged. Breathing can also affect how we feel. For example, people with anxiety usually learn that by taking some deep breaths for a few minutes, they can begin to calm themselves down and make better decisions. Sportswomen and men have used breathing for a long time to control aspects of health and training, such as power, and to improve vital components of fitness like speed and strength.

How can we use taking a breath?
We can use taking a breath for slowing down the heart rate in times of high emotion. Maybe someone has said something to us that is hurtful or untrue, or we may have just had a shock or heard some sad news. By controlling the breathing we can learn to think more clearly and view the situation in a calmer and more positive and way. Also, when exercising, breathing properly ensures the muscles get the correct amount of air and nutrients to support them.

FUNWORK
1. Identify how you are breathing right now. Is your breathing shallow or deep?

2. Take ten deep breaths in silence right now. Notice the difference in how your mind and body feel.

3. Identify three possible events in the future where you can use breathing techniques to remain calm.

1. _____

_____

2. _____

_____

3. _____

_____

U – UNDERSTANDING YOURSELF AND OTHERS

What is understanding yourself and others?

Understanding ourselves is critical to understanding others. If we do not know how we think or why we make the decisions we do, then we will not be able to develop empathy with others. Understanding ourselves also enables us to be more aware of the effects of our words and actions on others, as well as enabling others to get to know us better.

Where does it come from?

Understanding yourself comes from meditation, knowing your true values and beliefs in all areas in your life, practising slow breathing, being mindful in every moment possible and being aware of the mind–body connection. Understanding others comes from listening to them, making eye contact with them and not interrupting them while they communicate with you. It's always important to watch other people's body language, listen attentively to them and give them the space to truly express themselves without being judged.

How does understanding yourself and others affect you?

Understanding yourself affects everything you do. If you don't know how to align your actions with your real beliefs and values, then your life will simply not end up where you envisioned it. If you can understand others, you can help them with their problems and also see their perspective. If someone has a different perspective to you, it's important to be able to put yourself "in their shoes". This gives you a better understanding of how to respond to their speech or actions. If you understand the other person's point of view, it's much easier to find common ground and work with them.

How can you use this understanding in your life?

Rapport is a huge part of understanding yourself and others. If you lack rapport with yourself, then you may be "in two minds" about something. For example one part of you might want to be healthy, whilst the other part wants to eat two bars of chocolate. However, if you understand "why" you're having problems refusing the bars of chocolate and have an honest conversation with yourself, telling yourself "I am going to stay healthy with healthy choices" – that's called understanding yourself! Rapport with other people is also critical. If you can understand others, you will find it easier to talk to them, find common ground with them, and therefore get to the bottom of any problem.

FUNWORK
In what ways do you need to understand yourself better in each of the following areas?

Love

_____
_____
_____

Health

_____
_____
_____

Relationships

_____
_____
_____

V – VULNERABILITY

What is vulnerability?
Vulnerability is the ability to feel at peace with not being strong all the time and not always being in control. It's a place where most people feel very uncomfortable and it can feel disempowering and threatening.

Where does vulnerability come from?
Vulnerability comes from knowing that you may not always be as strong as you would like to think. It means being patient in difficult times and being honest with yourself and others (where appropriate) about your problems. You can then begin to work on your emotions and learn how to cope with new and difficult situations.

Why is vulnerability so powerful?
It's powerful because going into a vulnerable state, and feeling and accepting this odd emotion, is in fact a good thing. It is also very powerful for others to recognise this in you – it makes them see you are human and very real and helps them realise you have problems, just as they do.

How can we use vulnerability?

We can use vulnerability when we talk to people, letting them know how we feel if it's appropriate, and coming from a place in the mind which contains no ego. Vulnerability can be used to share feelings and experiences with people whom you trust.

FUNWORK

In which areas of your life do you feel vulnerable?

_____

_____

_____

_____

What steps can you take to feel less vulnerable in these areas?

_____

_____

_____

_____

W – WILLPOWER

What is willpower?

Willpower is our "why". The why is important to know and understand. It's our mission, our reason or purpose for doing something, especially when we are talking about a type of behaviour or a habit that we need to begin to repeat every day to achieve something we desire in life.

Where does the why come from?

The why comes from knowing our outcome will have a healthy, positive effect on our life. We realise there's a fantastic reason to achieve the goal we have set ourselves.

Why is willpower so powerful?

It's powerful because if what we want to achieve or find creates a burning desire in our mind, then the unconscious mind can support the conscious mind when it wants to use willpower. This motivation will drive us to accomplish our goal because it comes from within. Our own willpower and why are always far more powerful than an external motivator. The external why is like a warm shower – after a few hours the effects have already worn off. A classic example of an external motivator is a drill instructor barking orders at you – if you don't believe in what he is saying, you will just follow his orders until he stops shouting. An example of an internal motivation is a dream you have had since you were a child...maybe it was to fly a plane. Eventually you will find a way, whatever it takes, to earn money, save it up and be able to achieve that dream.

How can we use willpower?

The way we use our why is by recalling our goal each day. We can also give ourselves rewards as we move towards it. We need the why to drive the willpower – otherwise our dreams won't come true.

FUNWORK

What are your three current whys and willpower drivers in each of the following?

Relationships:
_____
_____
_____
_____

Health:
_____
_____
_____
_____

Business:
_____
_____
_____
_____

X – CROSS OUT THE NEGATIVE INFLUENCES IN YOUR LIFE

What is crossing out?
Crossing out is a way to eliminate the negative influences in your life. Examples of these influences are negative people, places and products, as well as television and alcoholic or sugary drinks. **Remember - show me your friends and I will show you your future!**

Where does crossing out come from?
This comes from the conscious mind deciding what has a positive influence on us and choosing to remove the negative influences by crossing them out of our life totally, to improve the quality of our lives.

Why is crossing out so important?
Crossing out negative influences is important because these influences affect us on an unconscious level – our mind is absorbing information at all times and we must understand that proximity is power. For example, if we are spending time with high-energy, healthy people we will probably become like them. But if we are spending time with friends who always complain

about their lives, we will probably follow them. Therefore the time we give them may need to be limited. Other external negative influences can also leave us feeling low and unhappy, as well as draining our energy, so we must replace them with positive ones.

How can we use crossing out?
We can use this by identifying all the negative influences in our life and then reducing our exposure to them. They range from friends to foods and can even include family members!

FUNWORK
Which three things do you need to cross out in your life or reduce your exposure to? Explain why for each one.

1. _____
_____
2. _____
_____
3. _____
_____

Y – YOUR TIME

What is your time?
Mindfulness is critical when it comes to time management. Time is a concept; however it's important to remember we all have the same amount of time. How we use time, therefore, is fascinating – people who use it wisely and mindfully achieve their outcomes far more easily than "time-wasters". Being mindful of time gives you more time. When you are aware of it, you can use it to much better effect. **Remember – You never find time, you must MAKE time.**

Why is time so important?
Time is important because it controls what we do with our day. The world we live in relies on the concept of time and most industrialised societies operate around the clock. We all have twenty-four hours a day to use and we have to be strategic with our time. Why do people who seem to enjoy life more have more time and how do they manage it? It's simply because these people allocate time in chunks to aspects of their daily lives, then commit themselves to different tasks.

Time management comes into play in our lives and becomes very powerful when we use time in ten-minute chunks. When we learn to allocate between ten and thirty minutes a day to different activities, many things can be accomplished. For example, just planning a ten-minute workout every day or making time for a simple ten-minute meditation has huge benefits for everyone.

How can we use time in an improved way?
We can use time better by creating a schedule for our day in the morning, and not beginning the day until our plans are written down on paper, with our outcomes and goals specified. Being more specific about how we intend to use our time during our twenty-four hours will help us identify which areas need the most focus and time.

FUNWORK

Write down how much time (in minutes or hours) every day you allocate to the following areas:

Health: _____

Meditation: _____

Your passion: _____

Relationship: _____

Fun: _____

Making money: _____

Z – ZONE

What is the zone?
The zone is a place in your mind where you can go by using a consciously chosen trigger (usually an external one). In the zone you feel happy, safe and confident. Being able to get to it helps you to improve your state of mind, and being in the zone enables us to accomplish our aims or overcome our difficulties.

Where is the zone?
The zone is in the unconscious mind and can be accessed by using various triggers. These include your favourite music, place or healthy food or drink, or the company of an amazing person who brings the best out of you.

Why is the zone so important?
The zone is important because it lets us inhabit a place within the mind that is emotionally strong and happy and from which we are able to respond to external events in a better and more positive fashion. It provides us with a stable environment to think and act from.

Most people get to the zone via alcohol, drugs or unhealthy processed foods –making them think they are happy. However, these provide only a short-term fix and unfortunately have longer-term negative health consequences.

How can you use the zone?

You can use the zone when you need to make decisions about relationships, business or health. For example, if we are feeling safe and secure, we will be able to avoid panic and reactivity, and so be able to respond more wisely to our challenges.

FUNWORK

Identify what trigger you can use to get into a happy zone from the following:

Music – which song?

_____

_____

_____

Which healthy food or drink?

_____

_____

_____

Which exercise – walking, weight-lifting, aerobics?

_____

_____

_____

Which memory can you go back to that puts you into your happy zone instantly?

_____

_____

_____

CONGRATULATIONS!

Now you have learnt the A to Z of mindfulness, simply focus on one letter per day for 26 days.

I recommend you study a letter of this book whenever you wake up and before falling to sleep, to enable your unconscious mind to process and absorb this.

WHERE OUR FOCUS GOES, ENERGY FLOWS!

SUMMARY

One of the most important aspects of mindfulness is that simply pausing for one second, breathing and living in the moment is a very powerful skill and one which we can all easily acquire. All we have to do then is apply it to our daily lives.

Most people live in the past or future and do not understand that it's the now that is the true present! It's a gift we have all been given, though we may not realise that.

By applying the lessons learnt from the funwork at the end of each letter's entry, you will see small shifts towards positive outcomes, and this will be felt, seen and heard during the rest of your life.

ABOUT THE AUTHOR

My name is Rick Parcell and I thought you might be interested in my motivation for writing this book – how it came into consciousness and how it was developed. So here is the story of my journey to mindfulness so far....

I grew up in a small, poor and quiet town by the sea in Yorkshire and always knew I had the potential to achieve anything in life. Unfortunately, as with many of us, the environment I grew up in simply did not support me and I feel it didn't allow me to discover my potential in many respects. Now don't get me wrong, I had a stable home and am grateful for that...my mother and father gave me good shelter, fed me, paid for and supported me on holidays! However, my school education and the limited and narrow mindset of many of my contemporaries and friends at the time did not serve me. This prevented me from finding my true consciousness and higher self. One man however, my grandfather, Captain Ron Wigley – kept my mindfulness high and my mind fully open.

I was not given many opportunities to find out who I really was and realise my true potential...

but then something happened...

My first change of consciousness – shipwrecked! I was shipwrecked in Greece at fifteen years old!

My grandfather, Captain Ron, asked me to join him on a yacht delivery trip in the Mediterranean in 1990. We sailed across the seas, beginning in Majorca, and stopping off at ports in Spain, Sardinia, Italy, Sicily and finally Greece. I didn't realise it at the time, but I was quickly switching from a closed mindset of lower consciousness and poor thinking, which I'd gained from the environment I had just come from, to a more expansive view of life. Captain Ron's bigger thinking about the world helped my mind to open like a flower and become more aware, and I began to find my true self. Different people, new cultures, new lands, new foods, new skills learned on the yacht, new languages picked up, new foods and new drinks – experiencing and accepting all these things changed my outlook for good!

To cut a long story short, we ended up shipwrecked on rocks at 2 a.m. on the shores of Greece! We were rescued by Greek fishermen and had to live for a week in a beautiful fishing village, eating fabulous Greek food and staying with lovely people in an amazing climate. At fifteen years old, this got me thinking, "If this environment is challenging my thinking and taking me out of my comfort zone in so many ways, where else can my mind go with experiences like these?"

My second change of consciousness – a seminar.

At seventeen years old, I saw another escape route out of my usual environment: the Royal Navy. I spent fourteen highly successful years in the navy (nine of them at sea) and quickly rose to Petty Officer Physical Trainer – basically developing myself and others every day, mentally and physically, and travelling the world on six different warships. I left in 2006 and began to teach underprivileged sixteen- to nineteen-year-olds life skills.

Then, in 2012, I went to a seminar that changed the course of my life, elevating my thinking to the next level, and for the second time I became more mindful. After this seminar, during which I went through many mind exercises and experiences, I promised myself I would learn something new for ten minutes a day for the rest of my life.

My third change of consciousness – The Body Camp guests.

In 2011, I began working at retreats and transforming people's lives by helping them build new daily habits and behaviour with their minds and bodies, and in 2016, I finally partnered up with four other positive people to create The Body Camp. This allowed me to make more use of my own ideas and creativity – which raised my consciousness for the third time in my life. I simply listened to everybody who attended the camp and created ways and methods to help them with their pain points, fears and worries.

Guests started to tell me that I should write a guidebook on mindfulness and I realised that by using each letter of the alphabet, I could explain to others how we can all achieve mindful living easily every day.

ACKNOWLEDGEMENTS

The journey to writing this book has been only 42 years in the making. I would like to mention and thank the following people.... I could not have done it without them.... First of all my mum, dad and sister, cousin Danny H and Lucy H in Switzerland for countless nights of life lessons and stories at their family home and of course Lucy H's incredible food which gave us the energy, whenever I am fortunate enough to be in their presence.. Mentor Jim N in San Francisco who's insights and guidance have been life changing. Frank L for his caring, family philosophy and sense of humor.. Shay O - who has been sensational in supporting my dreams and helping me find my dance shoes. Stacy W for supporting me, giving me incredible bandwidth to write and create this book in a safe, homely environment, despite outside pressures, and huge commitments.

Uncle Tony - for lessons in sport and ability. Annelise, Kathleen H in Switzerland and Diane B in Portsmouth - for fantastic advice and being powerful women role models to me. Captain Ron, my grandfather who opened my mind up to the world when I was young. Dave G and Shawn W in L.A. for advising me when I lived in L.A.. Cynthia P for handing me a gift in 2012 that changed my direction and Jazz M for being a good Yorkshire friend back then. Kate W and my other business partners Ben W and Jackie O for believing in my crazy methods and beliefs and for putting up with me at thebodycamp.com. Sofia G for helping me put this book together. Finally my best friend - Rebel, who helped me discover the innocent beauty of nature and the gift of life.

"The quality of your life simply depends on two things....

1. The quality of your thoughts.

2. Your communication... to yourself!"

R Parcell

'Mindfulness is simple when you focus and cut the crap'

Rick Parcell invites you to take the journey of consciousness in this easy to follow workbook.

"Rick was a Physical Training Instructor who helped the military get into top condition—physically, mentally and emotionally. Their lives depended on it. If you'd like to learn Mindfulness from a Master teacher, I highly recommend you read this." – Rich Litvin, founder of 4PC and Author of the book "The Prosperous Coach"

"Even now, more than a year after Rick left California to realise his dreams in Ibiza, when I workout without him, I hear his wisdom and encouragement in the back of my mind. I gained a friend, physical and mental mentor." – Frank Langen

CUT THE CRAP!
A YORKSHIRE MAN'S A-TO-Z GUIDE
TO MINDFULNESS

TWITTER @RICKPARCELL
FACEBOOK RICK PARCELL